CARTOONING

ART
FOR KIDS

CARTOONING

The Only Cartooning Book You'll Ever Need to Be the Artist You've Always Wanted to Be

Art Roche

LARK BOOKS

A Division of Sterling Publishing Co., Inc.
New York

Editor:
JOE RHATIGAN

Art Direction,
Design & Production:
CELIA NARANJO

Cover Illustration:
ART ROCHE

Editorial Assistance:
DELORES GOSNELL

Library of Congress Cataloging-in-Publication Data

Roche, Art.
  Cartooning : the only cartooning book you'll ever need to be the artist
you've always wanted to be / Art Roche.
      p. cm. — (Art for kids)
  Includes index.
  ISBN 1-57990-623-0 (hardcover)
  1. Cartooning—Technique—Juvenile literature. 2.
Drawing—Technique—Juvenile literature. I. Title. II. Series.
NC1320.R616 2005
741.5—dc22

                                    2004025440

10 9 8 7 6 5 4 3 2

Published by Lark Books, A Division of
Sterling Publishing Co., Inc.
387 Park Avenue South, New York, N.Y. 10016

Distributed in Canada by Sterling Publishing,
c/o Canadian Manda Group, 165 Dufferin Street
Toronto, Ontario, Canada M6K 3H6

Distributed in the United Kingdom by GMC Distribution Services,
Castle Place, 166 High Street, Lewes, East Sussex, England BN7 1XU

Distributed in Australia by Capricorn Link (Australia) Pty Ltd.,
P.O. Box 704, Windsor, NSW 2756 Australia

If you have questions or comments about this book, please contact:
Lark Books
67 Broadway
Asheville, NC 28801
(828) 253-0467

Manufactured in China

ISBN 13: 978-1-57990-623-8
ISBN 10: 1-57990-623-0

For information about custom editions, special sales, premium and corporate purchases,
please contact Sterling Special Sales Department at 800-805-5489 or specialsales@sterlingpub.com.

Contents

Introduction

CARTOONISTS CAN DO AMAZING THINGS. Who else can create animals that talk or superheroes that can bend steel bars with their bare hands? A cartoonist simply grabs a pencil and lets his or her imagination run wild. I've been drawing and doodling since I was a little kid, and today I'm still drawing cartoons. In fact, it's my job. I make a living doing something I love!

Imagine the amazing characters you can create!

Bunny Guy. Action hero and acknowledged cartoon expert.

I'LL BE YOUR OFFICIAL CARTOONING TOUR GUIDE.

That's why I'm so excited to present my very own cartooning book. This is the book I wish I had as a kid. Why? Well, there are plenty of cartooning books out there that show you how to draw famous cartoon characters and imitate other cartoonists' styles, but that's not what real cartooning is. *This book is about developing your own characters and style.* It's all about you! You learn the basics and then let your imagination take over. I also included cool information about writing jokes (drawing cartoons is only half the fun) and getting published (it's awesome to have an audience).

So whether you want to learn some neat cartooning tricks for your doodles or create a collection of cartoons to launch your career, this book is for you. It was fun to write and draw it, and I know you'll have fun reading and drawing along.

Art Roche

Chapter 1
Cartoons Everywhere!

Cartoon: a simplified representation of a humorous situation.

TRANSLATION: A CARTOON IS A FUNNY DRAWING.

NOW, IF YOU'RE INTO COMIC BOOKS, you know that cartoons don't always have to be funny. For the most part, however, cartoons are fun to draw and create, and they also make people laugh (or at least smile). Before we start looking for and developing that cartoonist we all know is in you, let's take a moment to discuss a few of the more popular forms of cartooning.

You'll find that the cartooning activities in this book can help you with any type of cartoon out there, but the examples we use the most fall into five categories: comic strips, gag cartoons, advertising cartoons, comic books, and doodling.

Comic Strips

Look through your local daily newspaper and you'll find one of the coolest ways to draw cartoons: the comic strip. As the name says, the comic strip is a strip of panels (usually three or four) that tells a visual story. It's usually a short conversation between characters or a quick bit of action. Most comic strips these days are funny and have a punch line at the end. With a little bit of practice, you can draw your own comic strips. They can be really fun because you get to write your own stories and create a cast of characters.

A **PUNCH LINE** IS THE LAST LINE OF A JOKE THAT MAKES YOU LAUGH (IF THE JOKE IS A GOOD ONE).

HOW DO YOU LIKE MY NEW CAR?

Set up your situation. The first character talks.

NOT BAD BUNNY GUY. DOES IT GET GOOD MILEAGE?

The second character talks, reacting to what the first character said.

25 HOPS TO THE GALLON.

This is the punch line! It can be a clever twist of words or a really unexpected reaction. It needs to be surprising.

Gag Cartoons

Dear, we're running low on carrots.

Gag cartoons have one funny picture, usually square shaped, with some text under the picture to complete the joke. The drawing is the first thing readers will see, and then they'll read the text. The text is called the *caption*.

Gag cartoons can be fun because there are a zillion different jokes you can tell with the same drawing. It just depends on how you change the caption. Cover up the caption above and think of your own. Because of the simple and fun nature of gag cartoons, many of the examples in this book use gag cartoons for practice. They are a great place to start.

Advertising Cartoons

Next time you're in the supermarket, go down the aisles and count the cartoons you see on boxes and packaging. You might see a hundred cartoon drawings in the cereal aisle alone. Think of your favorite kind of cereal. It probably has a cartoon character on the front of every box. See? Cartoons are everywhere!

Have some fun while you're eating breakfast. Look at the front of your cereal box and try to draw the cartoon character. Copying a cartoon character is great practice.

Comic Books, POW!

Everyone knows what a comic book is. We've all seen superhero comic books in grocery stores, bookstores, and comic book shops. They're small, multipage stories and are usually printed in full color. Because they're a longer format than other types of cartooning, they require a different kind of storytelling. Page layouts, story flow, and characters become much more important in a comic book. Comic books are really illustrated novels, and they require a well-developed talent for writing good stories. If you want to tell longer, action-oriented stories, or if you want to create your own superhero, then you might be well suited for comic books.

TELL LONGER STORIES IN COMIC BOOK FORM.

Doodling

Now we come to the type of cartooning that everyone has fun with: doodling. Who hasn't picked up a pen while on the phone and started scribbling on a sheet of scrap paper? If your only reason for reading this book is to get better at doodles, that is reason enough! Cartooning should be a fun, carefree activity, and doodling is the most fun of all! So "doodle on," my friend—no further instructions required.

Chapter 2
Cartooning Materials

DON'T WORRY. You don't need a bunch of expensive pencils and erasers or some special kind of paper to draw cartoons. Thirty thousand years ago, cave dwellers did it with sticks and berry juice on stone walls! You probably have everything you need in your home already. If not, your local pharmacy or office supply store will have the modern tools you need. Don't feel any pressure to buy the highest quality materials, either. It's more important that you begin drawing now and start having fun. Over time you'll grow to love one brand of tool over another. For now, however, let's start with the basics.

Pencils

Pencils come in many shapes and sizes. First, there's the standard wooden pencil that you've used since kindergarten, as well as the more modern mechanical pencil with replaceable leads. You can use either one to draw your cartoons.

Pencil leads come in varying shades of darkness, depending on how they're manufactured at the factory. This darkness factor is given a number (or letter) code. That's why the teacher asks you to bring a "number-two pencil" to class. The number two signifies a pencil with a #2 lead. This is the standard lead found in almost all pencils, and it's fine for cartooning. The other two popular sizes are 2B and HB.

HB = Harder lead. Creates a thinner, lighter line.

#2 = Medium weight. Creates a medium, dark line.

2B = Soft lead. Good if you need a thick, dark line.

Paper

Of course, every cartoonist needs paper. Any kind of blank paper will do, but try to avoid notebook paper with the blue lines on it. Those lines can be distracting, and the final product won't look as neat and polished as clean white drawing paper. Most discount stores carry a selection of affordable, spiral-bound drawing pads.

Erasers

Even professional cartoonists need to erase all the time. Make sure your pencils have nice soft erasers. You may want to buy a small block eraser for erasing large areas.

A kneaded eraser has the texture of soft clay and won't damage your paper while you're erasing. It's good for removing light pencil lines after you've drawn over your cartoon with a pen. You can keep this soft rubbery eraser clean by pulling it apart over and over again.

Keeping It All Straight

Cartooning is all about loose, funny drawings. Sometimes, though, you'll need to draw clean, straight lines. So get a 12-inch ruler, and once you really get into cartooning, consider buying a T-square. This strange-looking tool can be found at most art supply stores. A 24-inch T-square should do the trick.

To use a T-square, line up the edge of the crossbar with the edge of your sketchpad or table. This lets you draw straight lines across the paper. If you draw very lightly in pencil, you can easily erase these lines later. You can also purchase a triangle to draw diagonal and vertical lines.

Pens

Pens come in all weights, thicknesses, and styles. Almost any good black pen will be okay for cartooning, but many of the pens below are popular with experienced cartoonists. Buy a few of these pens and try them out. It's important to choose one that feels right to you. As you become more experienced, you may want to use permanent ink that won't fade over time. Until then, just choose a pen and go for it.

Standard ballpoint pen. You probably have one of these in a kitchen drawer somewhere. It's fine to use, but the line isn't very thick and it won't reproduce well on a photocopy machine.

Felt-tip marker. This is a good choice for a beginner. The ink usually isn't permanent, but it gives a nice, thick, dark line, and it's easy to control. Choose a "thin" or "very thin" tip.

Drafting pen. This type of pen gives a very even and smooth line. It usually has permanent, good-quality ink. These pens come in a variety of line widths. Look for a width of .80 or 1.0 for cartooning.

Brush pen. This handy little pen comes with a brushlike tip built in. This is great for practicing a smooth thick or thin line weight in your drawings. Try to find one with permanent ink, because some of them will smudge when exposed to moisture.

Quill pen. This is the granddaddy of all cartooning pens. Many professional cartoonists use one. You dip the metal tip into an ink jar and draw until the ink runs out. Then you dip it again. It sounds like a chore, but you can get beautiful line quality with a pen like this. You may have to look in an art supply store for one of these babies. Usually the tips and the pen holders are sold separately.

Now that we've gotten rid of those prehistoric sticks and berry-juice inks, grab a pencil and some paper and get started!

PENS

Chapter 3
Making Faces

ENOUGH WITH THE SMALL TALK. Let's start by drawing cartoon faces! Remember, a cartoonist's job is to be funny or tell good stories using as few lines as possible. Good cartoon faces are simple and easy to look at. They are not supposed to be detailed works of fine art. Sure, some cartoonists use more detail than others, but there's nothing wrong with drawing a plain circle for a head and two dots for the eyes. So relax and keep it simple.

Cool.   **Just as cool.**

As you work on your faces, try new combinations of styles and designs until you have something you really like. Choose the face parts that you like best and keep practicing with those. I hope you'll do more than just trace the cartoons on these pages. By the end of this chapter, you may already have some characters of your very own.

For the next six pages you'll get the chance to work with some unfortunate cartoon characters that are missing face parts. Grab a pencil and your drawing paper and give them a hand...err...a face!

Give Me Some Eyes

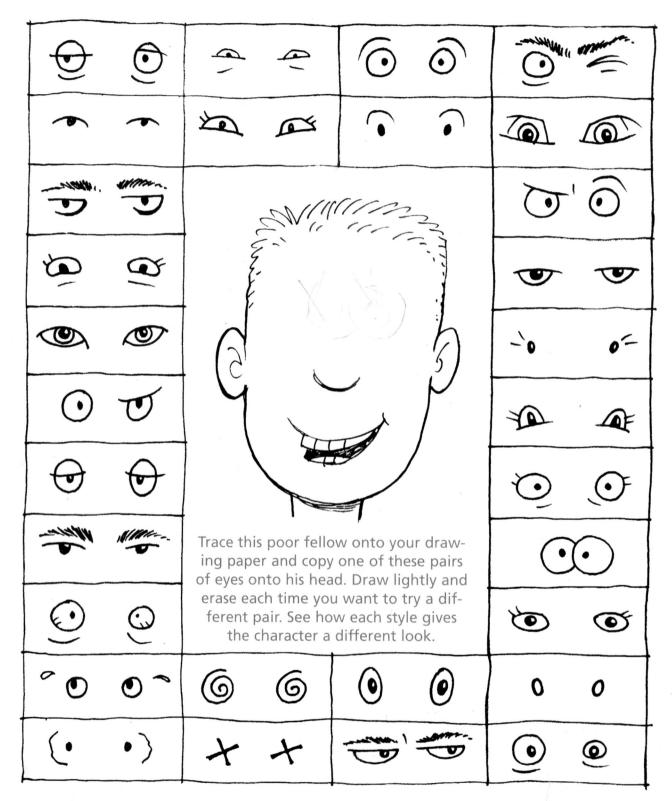

Trace this poor fellow onto your drawing paper and copy one of these pairs of eyes onto his head. Draw lightly and erase each time you want to try a different pair. See how each style gives the character a different look.

I Smell Awful

Trace this unfortunate girl and try out some noses on her. Which nose looks best? Make up a few of your own if you want. You're the artist.

Ears Looking at You

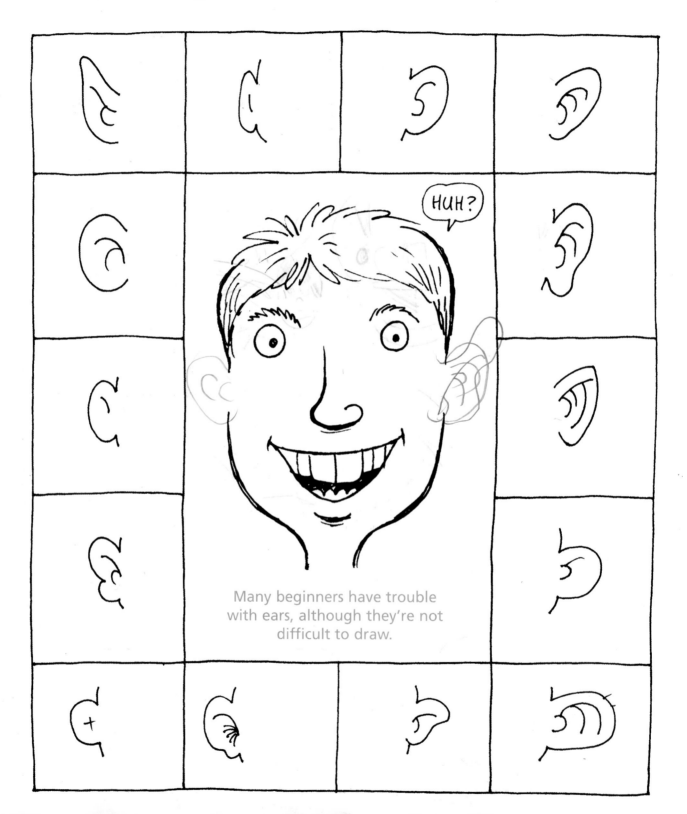

Many beginners have trouble with ears, although they're not difficult to draw.

Lip Service

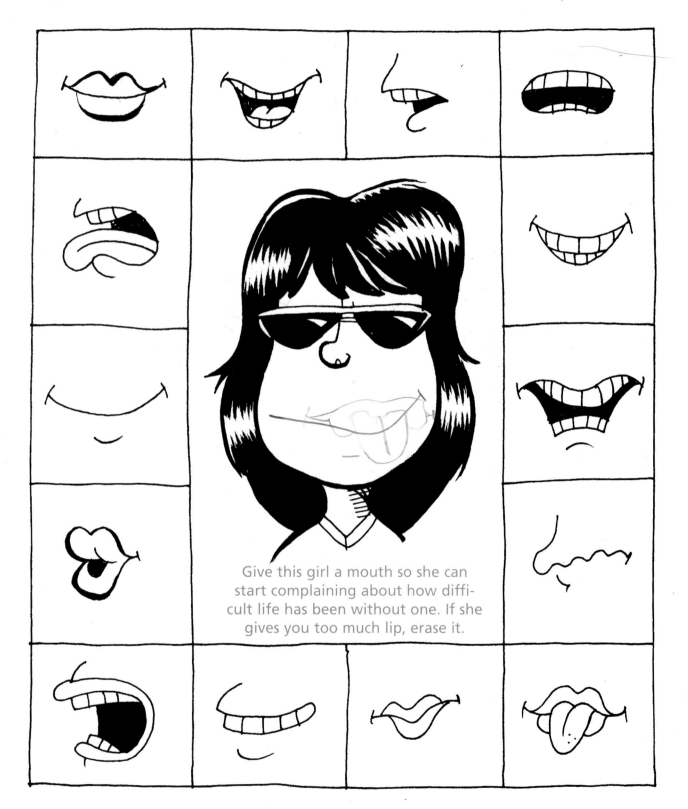

Give this girl a mouth so she can start complaining about how difficult life has been without one. If she gives you too much lip, erase it.

Hair Today, Gone Tomorrow

Adding hair can be as simple as drawing a single line or as complicated as drawing lots of lines.

Putting It All Together

Here are some heads in need of faces. Trace the heads onto some drawing paper and practice different combinations of eyes, noses, mouths, and ears. Remember: Keep it simple.

Now, On Your Own

With your pencil, begin by blocking out the general shape of the head. Most heads are oval or egg-shaped, but of course, you can play with the head's dimensions.

Once you have your head shape, draw a line down the center of the face and a line across the middle of the face, or where you want the eyes to go. These lines help keep the face symmetrical (even on both sides). Make a simple oval for the nose and a couple of dots where the eyes will go. Mark where the mouth and ears will go.

Begin to carve out the character's face, picking a nose, eyes, mouth, and ears. Keep sketching until you're happy with the face. Don't forget hair!

Put your finished sketch up to a window and turn it over. The sketch should look good on both sides of the paper. If your drawing passes this test, you have a winner of a face. If not, give it another try.

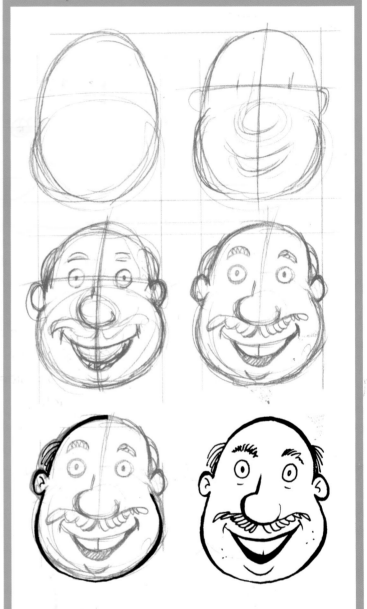

Turn Your Cartoon Heads Around

In cartoons, you probably won't be drawing your characters directly from the front. Most drawings show the characters turned slightly to the left or right. This is because your characters are talking to each other, not looking straight ahead. You'll need to get used to drawing heads from different angles.

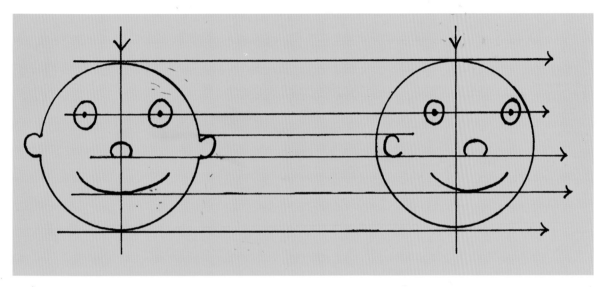

Start with a character looking straight at you. Then, to turn it a little to the side, simply draw horizontal lines through the main features. Following the lines, slide the eyes, nose, and mouth a little to one side. After some practice you'll be able to draw your characters from any angle!

Choose some of the faces you've drawn so far and move them around to get the hang of drawing faces in different positions.

Changing Expressions

Check this out! If you want to change your cartoon face's expression, all you need are a few simple marks for a complete makeover. We'll start with this happy young chap and begin to change a few lines. Watch the dramatic results. I hope this guy doesn't mind.

Adding some mad eyebrows and few wrinkle marks above the nose really makes this guy seem mean—like a bully. When you combine a smile with mad eyebrows, your character will usually look mean or cruel.

Make his eyebrows lighter, and tilt them down on the ends like this, and suddenly the same face looks afraid or worried. Try this yourself using a simple smiley face and different combinations of eyebrows. Fascinating, isn't it?

Here's a strange one. Tilt one eyebrow into a worried look and the other at an angry angle, and now you have someone who looks clever or devious. Watch out for this guy; he'll cheat you out of your lunch money.

When you draw the eyes half closed and raise the eyebrows, your character will look sleepy or slow. If you want a character to look not very alert, always draw him with his eyes half open.

Adding lines to a face also begins to age the character. Notice the wrinkles around the eyes and on both sides of the mouth. You only need to add a few lines to make your characters seem much older. Don't use too many, because your character's face should be easy to see.

From "In Your Head" to "On the Page"
(in Three Simple Steps)

This is a good place to chat about the three basic steps you'll use to create all the cartoon drawings you'll do in this book. Most professional cartoonists take these steps for granted, but for the beginner, practicing them can make a huge difference in the quality of your drawings.

Step 1. PLAN: With a pencil, draw the rough basic shapes of your cartoon. At this point, you don't care how sloppy it looks.

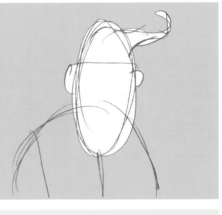

Step 2. SKETCH: Still using your pencil, begin adding details on top of your basic shapes. Your sketch might still be sort of messy. No worries!

Step 3. INK: With your pen, draw right on top of the pencil lines—choosing the best lines as you go. When you're done, carefully erase the pencil marks.

The Three-Step Plan in Action

Plan It!

Block out your cartoon on the page using simple shapes. Drawing very lightly with a pencil, decide where all of the shapes look best in your cartoon. The arrangement of these shapes is called the *composition*. Don't worry about being sloppy or making mistakes. Some professional cartoonists like to sketch using a light blue colored pencil. Light blue pencil doesn't show up as much in a photocopy, so it sometimes requires less erasing.

Sketch It!

Start drawing the details of your cartoon right on top of the rough shapes. Continue using a light pencil line so that you can clean up the drawing later. Draw all the funny details that will go into your cartoon. Go over each line more than once, until you get exactly the drawing you want.

Ink It!

The last step is finishing your drawing. This is most commonly called inking, because so many cartoonists draw their finished cartoons in black permanent ink. Your sketch may be quite messy, with more than one line to choose from as you're inking. That's normal. Just pick the best line as you go, and trace over it neatly. The ink lines don't have to be perfect. Little wobbles and wiggles can give the drawing some life. Remember to keep your lines simple and easy to see, with not too much detail. After you're happy with the ink drawing, wait a few minutes to make sure that the ink is completely dry. Use your eraser to go over your cartoon carefully and erase all those crazy pencil sketch lines. You're left with a neat, clean cartoon drawing. Congratulations!

SEE PAGE 95 IF YOU WANT TO COLOR IN YOUR CARTOONS.

Let Your Imagination Go WILD

So far, you've picked out and drawn some cartoon face parts. You've learned the three steps in making a cartoon drawing. Now it's time to jump in and try it on your own. Below you'll find some descriptions of cartoon characters. Start drawing these characters on a separate piece of paper. For now, just concentrate on drawing the heads. We'll move on to cartoon bodies in the next chapter. Start with a simple oval, and then begin sketching in the details. Use your imagination. When your drawing starts to look really cool, you're done. Then you can go over the pencil lines with ink.

- Draw a mean pirate named Deadeye Blacktooth. He has a big broken nose, he has a patch over one eye, and he wears a scarf around his head. Make him as mean and scary as you want.

- Draw a smart teenage girl with gigantic hair and really long eyelashes. Give her a necklace and freckles.

- Draw a nice picture of someone in your family. Choose one of the cartoon eyes shown at the beginning of the chapter. Give the cartoon to him or her as a gift.

- Draw an alien creature from planet Zborff. Give him four eyes (or more) and some antennae on his head. Also give him a big smile, so he's not too scary.

- Draw a superhero with a big chin and a really thick neck. Give him or her dark wavy hair and bushy eyebrows and a name that starts with "Captain."

- Draw a little girl with her hair in pigtails. Make her mouth wide open, like she's yelling at someone. Give her some angry eyebrows, too. She's throwing a tantrum.

- Draw your teacher. Don't get caught!

- Draw yourself.

Chapter 4
Drawing Bodies

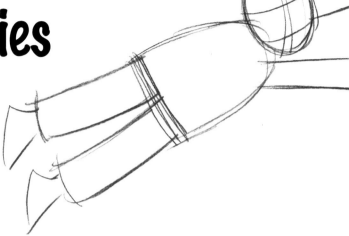

NOW THAT YOU'VE DRAWN some cool cartoon faces, let's start working on the rest of the picture… namely, cartoon bodies. Did you know that complex poses can be broken down into a few simple shapes? You don't need detailed anatomy lessons to draw a cool cartoon body. The most important part of drawing cartoon bodies is to communicate the action and emotion of your character as quickly and simply as possible.

Cartoon Anatomy

Here are the only shapes you really need to create bodies for all the cool faces you drew in Chapter 3.

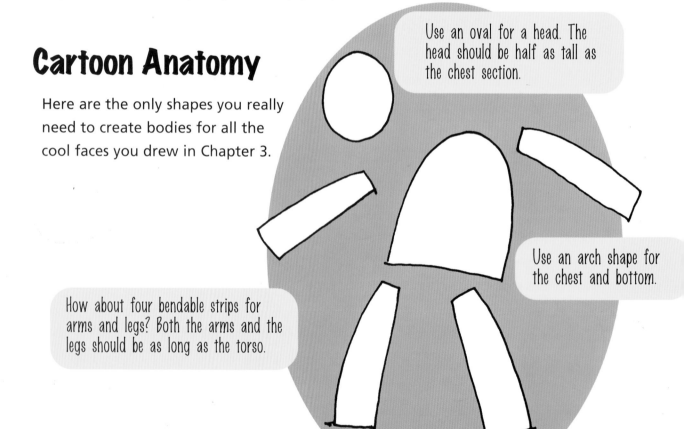

Use an oval for a head. The head should be half as tall as the chest section.

Use an arch shape for the chest and bottom.

How about four bendable strips for arms and legs? Both the arms and the legs should be as long as the torso.

Body Language

Planning, sketching, and inking come into play when figuring out a body's position. Things such as posture and attitude can be communicated with the body language illustrated in these funny little scribbles. You're like a director, posing your characters on the stage. You can put them in any position you want.

Try a few of these on a separate sheet of paper. On the following two pages, I show more ways to use these simple shapes and make an endless variety of poses.

More Body Language

Practice these positions and create some of your own.

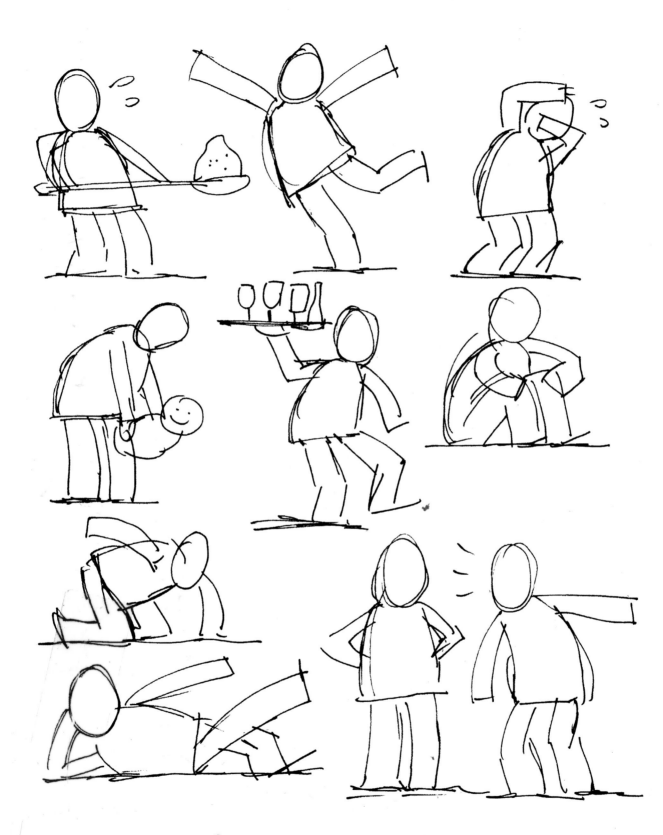

Balance

Pay attention to balance, particularly in these early planning drawings. Because your early drawings are the foundation of the final cartoon, they have to look balanced. If your character is supposed to be standing up on his own, you should be able to draw an imaginary line straight down, from the base of the character's neck to the heel of the supporting leg. If you don't balance your drawing, your character will always look like he's about to fall over.

In the examples at the bottom of this page, the guy on the left looks balanced and steady on his feet. By contrast, the poor fellow on the right looks like he's about to fall over. If you actually want the pose to be crazy and full of action, throw off the balance on purpose.

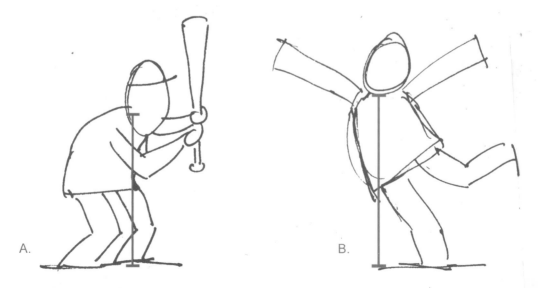

A.

B.

Planning, Sketching, and Inking Bodies

Shown below are the three stages of cartoon drawing: planning, sketching, and inking.

In the first stage, you can start with the very simple shapes shown on page 36.

Then, when you begin sketching your cartoon, fill in the detail right on top of the original shapes. That's why it's important to sketch lightly in pencil until you're really happy with the drawing. Finally, ink the final drawing.

Body Types

The world of cartoons is just like the real world in that people come in all shapes and sizes. The simple shapes you use to create the pose of your character can vary according to body type.

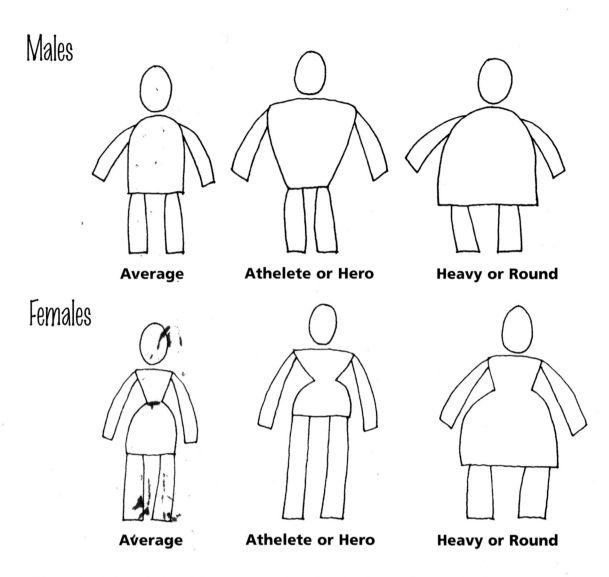

Males

Average

Athelete or Hero

Heavy or Round

Females

Average

Athelete or Hero

Heavy or Round

The principles of sketching poses using simple shapes is exactly the same as what you practiced on page 38, but you can use different shapes to represent all types of characters. I've shown some common body types used in most cartoons. Now, it's up to you. Try drawing some quick shape sketches using the body types above. Practice by creating some of the following:

• A superhero with his arms out in front, flying through the air
• A really heavy man balancing on one foot and holding an umbrella
• A woman running and jumping over a low fence

Remember, your drawing doesn't have to be perfect. Just have fun. After you're happy with these poses, keep drawing. Develop the sketch with more details until you think it's finished. Hey, look at you; you're a cartoonist!

Give Your Cartoons a Hand ... or Two

Drawing hands frustrates even professional cartoonists from time to time. The human hand is a miraculous and complex piece of machinery. Well, forget that! If we break the hand down into simple shapes, drawing it is easier. Again, we're not trying for a fine art rendering of the hand. We just want a simple outline that communicates quickly to the viewer. Simplicity is king.

You can start with a circle at the end of the arm. Then add a thumb so you know which way the hand is facing.

After that, just add four fingers at the top. The middle finger is taller than the index finger. The pinky is the shortest of the four. Keep these rules in mind and you won't go wrong. For practice, you can copy some of the hands on the next page until you get the hang of it.

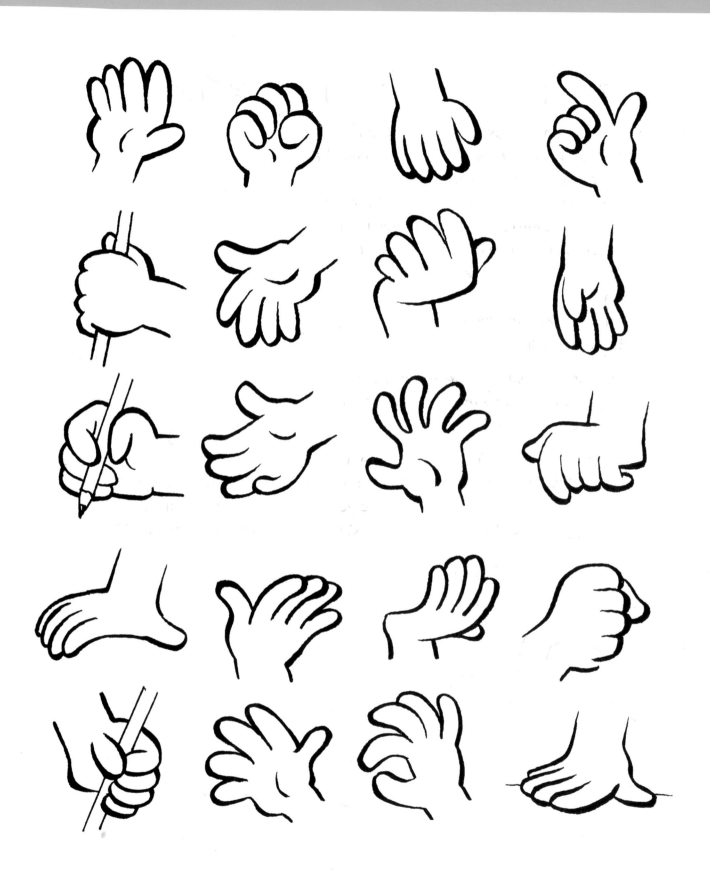

Drawing Feet

Pee-eew, stinky feet! Yes, even feet can be a chore to draw. However, broken down to its simplest shape, a foot is nothing but a triangle, with most of its point out in front and a little bit hanging off the back.

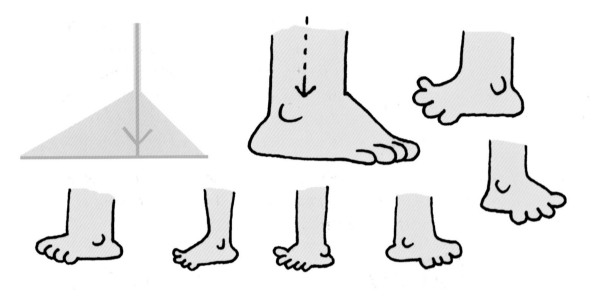

Draw a straight line directly down from the leg. That's the point that should support all the weight. Remember our balance line on page 40? Below, I've drawn some feet with shoes on. See? Feet can be fun. And easy!

Chapter 5
Drawing Stuff

OKAY, YOU'VE DRAWN SOME FUNNY FACES AND SOME ORIGINAL CHARACTERS. But cartooning is not just about people. This chapter looks at drawing everyday objects. In cartoons, objects are very often the props used to help tell the joke. If your cartoon needs to show a woman holding a frying pan, the joke won't work if you can't draw a frying pan. Sometimes an object is the most important piece of your cartoon. That's why it has to be easy to see and recognize.

As with cartoon people, the secret here is to simplify what you draw. Below and on the next page you'll see some photographs of real objects and the much simpler, cartoon versions of the same items.

Simplify!

(As if you didn't know this already.)

Don't try to copy every line of an object. In fact, if you look closely, you'll see that objects around us don't have any real lines at all! Your drawing only needs to communicate the basic shape.

Practice with some of the following examples, and then walk through your house drawing a few of your own. Keep your drawings simple and fun to look at.

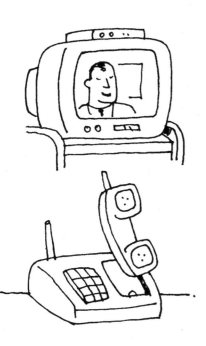

Give It a Try!

Draw the two objects below in a cartoon style. Leave out any detail that isn't absolutely necessary to identify what the objects are. Can you think of a cartoon that might include one (or both) of these objects?

Sometimes you can take a complex object, such as a car, and break it down into basic simple shapes the same way we did with cartoon people. Everything can be simplified. Just squint your eyes, and pick out the shapes you see. Don't get discouraged if you have trouble drawing complex things at first. Take your sketchbook with you wherever you go and practice drawing objects. Practice drawing people...practice drawing everything!

Objects in Cartoons

Here's a cartoon strip I did a few years ago. I wanted to show that the two people were in a coffee house. I drew the table and coffee cups. I drew the plant and storefront window behind the characters. I drew the date book that the woman is holding. All these objects, though not part of the joke itself, helped tell the joke by placing the situation in an environment. Objects and setting are important.

One flea collar, please.

Here's another example of placing the cartoon in the right setting. In this case, I wanted to show a man and his dog in a veterinarian's office or pet supply store, shopping for a flea collar. I showed very few details, just enough to tell the story.

Here's an example of the same cartoon, but this time I included a lot of unnecessary objects. Notice how the extra objects can be distracting. They help establish the setting, but this is just too much!

One flea collar, please.

Compare the cartoon above with the original version. Without all the extras, the reader's eye is directed right to the dog, where the joke is (a giant flea attached to the dog's rear end). Look at both cartoons now. Do you think the second cartoon has too many details?

Part of the cartoon planning process is creating your picture layout so that the most important object (the joke) is center stage and gets the most attention. Figuring out this stuff becomes part of the planning and sketching process when you begin drawing the cartoon.

Get Drawing Already!

Here's an activity to help you practice drawing objects. Listed below are some common items. Take out your sketchpad and read down the list. Can you draw each item from memory? If not, go and find one of the objects and really look at it. Think about how you can communicate with a few lines what that object looks like.

If your friends and family can look at your drawing and guess what all these objects are, you're on your way!

fork
spoon
bucket
spiral-bound notebook
glass with a straw in it
baseball cap
shovel

scissors
hammer
dump truck
floor lamp
window with
   curtains
television
frying pan

apple
pencil
soda can
telephone
computer
coffee mug
toothbrush

Start a Reference File

Many professional cartoonists save pictures of objects to use as reference. Just look through any old magazines, and cut out pictures of things that could be useful later. Keep these pictures in a file. That way, when you need to know what a computer or a lawn mower looks like, you can just pull out your file of pictures and take a look.

Adding a Dimension

Many cartoons are just black lines with colors filled in. People and objects in the real world, however, have shape and mass. In cartooning you have to imitate life using simples black lines and *shading*.

Shading is basically the illustration of the shadows created by shining a light source on something. The example to the right shows a plain round ball with and without shading added. It's hard to tell if the one on top is a ball ... or a pancake! Shading helps to communicate the roundness of the form. As you become a better cartoonist you'll want to add some shading to your drawings because it makes your cartoons look more solid.

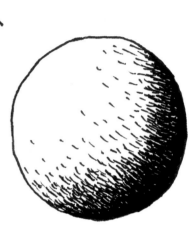

See how shading helps indicate curves and solid shapes in the drawing below?

These three bars show the process of creating shading.

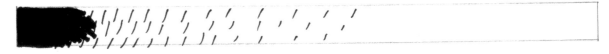

Start with the area of your object that's farthest away from the light and fill in a small area of black.

Then add small lines that get thinner and farther apart as you move away from the black shadow area.

Keep adding lines until you have a smooth transition from light to dark.

Experiment with different ways to add shading. Don't use too much— shading is best when it's used sparingly.

You can use little sketchy marks.

Or you can use scribbly marks.

How about criss-crossed lines? This is called _cross-hatching_.

Perspective

Before we conclude this section on drawing objects, let's look at the concept of *perspective* in your cartoons. Perspective is a way of drawing objects so that part of the object appears to be closer to the viewer, and part of the object appears to be further away. This comes in handy when you're using buildings or street scenes in your cartoons.

Start by using a ruler to draw a straight line across the page. Then mark a dot on the line off to one side. The straight line is called the *horizon line*, the dot is called the *vanishing point*. If you use the ruler again, and draw two more lines starting at the vanishing point and going off in two directions, you can begin to see what looks like a wall. It starts at the vanishing point (way off in the distance) and gets bigger as it gets closer to you. See the little guy next to the wall? You can also use these guide lines to make characters seem further away by having them get smaller and smaller as they approach the vanishing point. You can even create a box shape using a vanishing point on a horizon line.

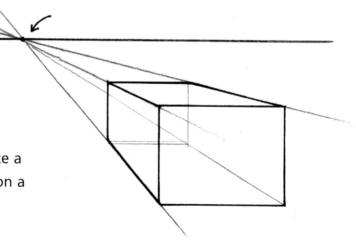

Using a horizon line with more than one vanishing point, you can create shapes with more than one side both above and below the horizon line. But who wants to just draw boxes?

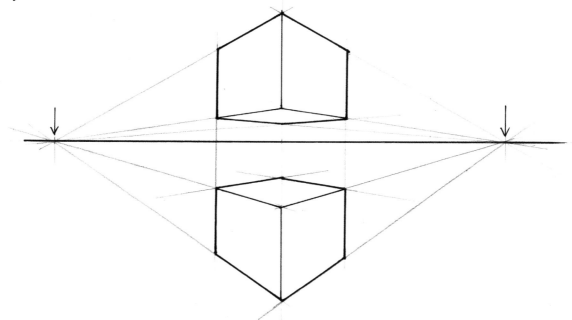

Using perspective gets really fun when you start using these principles to create complex 3-D structures and settings for your cartoons. Comic book artists are the best at using perspective in telling their stories. Pick up any action or adventure comic book, and you'll see a ton of great examples of dynamic perspective.

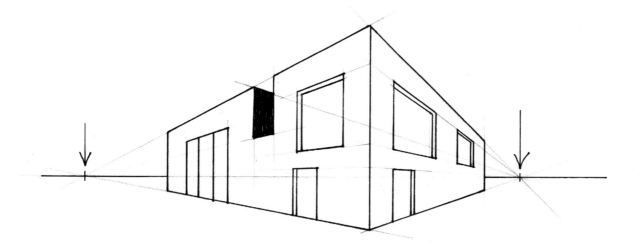

Chapter 6
Drawing Animals

FINALLY WE'VE REACHED THE SECTION ON DRAWING CARTOON ANIMALS. Animals can be funny, too. They can be real or imaginary. Basically, they can be anything you want! But just like cartoon people and cartoon objects, cartoon animals begin life as simple shapes on your paper. Four-legged animals start as a box shape. Remember to keep your drawings light and loose until you get into the sketching stage.

On the next few pages you'll see examples of simple shapes that suggest animals. All are a variation on the same design—a box with legs!

DOG

CAT

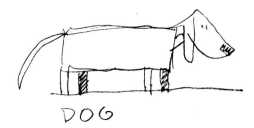

DOG

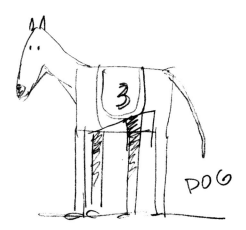

DOG

BEAR

No box needed here.

ELEPHANT

TIGER

ALLIGATOR

CAT

HIPPOPOTAMUS

Heads Up

Although you can start all four-legged animal bodies with a simple box shape, the head shapes actually vary quite a bit from one animal to the next. Study pictures of animals to get the feel for drawing their heads. Pictured here are simple head shapes for a cat, a dog, a horse, and a bear.

For the Birds

Birds are a different matter altogether. Start your bird drawings by lightly sketching the capital letter "D." Tilt the "D" downward, so that the round part of the "D" becomes the bird's belly. Now just add a small head and some skinny legs and you're in the bird business!

Draw Some Animals

Drawing cartoon animals takes practice and patience. Start with photographs if you need to, but remember to simplify along the way. Cut out any details that you don't need. Each of these drawings started out with a light sketch and slowly worked its way toward a finished cartoon drawing. Take out your sketch paper and try to redraw these animals, starting with a light sketch.

Start a Zany Zoo

Who says your cartoon animals have to look like anything at the zoo? This is cartooning! Get a laugh from your friends by making up completely new creatures. You're the artist; create new animals and make up your own names for them. Try combining two real animals, then mix up the two real names to form a silly new species.

NO RULES

Chapter 7
Writing Jokes

UP UNTIL NOW, we've been talking about the drawing side of being a cartoonist, but sometimes that's only half the story. Lots of cartoonists write as well as draw. So let's talk about writing.

A good cartoonist, much like a good writer, walks around all day looking for things that would make a cool story or an awesome idea. Your job is to keep your sketchpad with you at all times. Jot down ideas; make little sketches that record the world around you. You're looking for what's funny. The million-dollar question is: What does "funny" mean? Let's take a look, shall we?

What is Humor, Anyway?

Because you're the writer, the things you'll be looking for are the things that make you laugh. Did you laugh today or yesterday? Try and remember what it was that made you laugh...or even smile. Most people laugh at things that contain a portion of the three magical ingredients of humor: surprise, exaggeration, and the pairing of unlike objects or ideas. That sounds pretty technical, so I'll break it down a bit.

Surprise

People laugh at the unexpected. Many cartoons simply show a situation that is very unexpected, such as slipping on a banana peel or dropping a birthday cake. Try taking a normal situation and turning it around. How about a dog sitting in an armchair reading the newspaper while a man fetches the dog's slippers? Look for situations at home or school that can be turned around like this. That is surprise.

Exaggeration

With exaggeration, you start with a normal situation and embellish something to a ridiculous degree. Does your school backpack ever feel too heavy? Then draw it as big as a house, with you as a tiny little figure underneath the enormous weight. Have fun and use your imagination. Be silly. When the weather is hot, draw yourself melting. When it's cold, draw yourself as an ice cube. Does your little sister cry a lot? Draw a cartoon showing her flooding the entire house with tears…and you, waist deep in the water.

The Pairing of Unlike Objects or Ideas

Take two ideas that would never go together and…put them together. Start with a very serious environment, such as the operating room in a hospital. Then draw a clown in place of a surgeon. You'd never expect to see a clown there. Practically any punch line you write will be funny. This idea is closely related to using surprise, except that you're combining two unrelated ideas to get the surprise. How about an octopus showing up in your bedroom? Or the President of the United States roller-skating down the hall?

Start with something you think is funny. Then try to use one of these three methods to come up with an idea. Sometimes a combination of these techniques works best of all.

The Un-funny Life

I've had people tell me that their life isn't funny. I have to admit that I've felt that way myself. Everyone does. But looking for funny is an attitude. You have to open yourself up to the world around you. It takes practice to tune your funny-seeking radar. Don't get discouraged if you have trouble at first. Everyone does. Just keep trying and you'll soon start seeing everything through different eyes. All I can offer is one simple clue:

People are funniest when they're being human. They're most human when things go wrong. That means that you might find humor when simple, little things are wrong or out of place. That happens every day, right?

Here are a few common examples:

- An overgrown front yard
- A homemade cake gone wrong
- A bad hair day
- A leak in the plumbing
- A doomed science project
- A really messy room
- Dad making dinner
- A new kitten destroying furniture
- Losing the TV remote
- Jumping on the bed
- A dog that's too fat

Look for little things like this in your own life. Look for the weird, the out-of-place, the ridiculous. Start thinking about what a book of your cartoons would look like if you put all those funny little moments on paper.

Now, think of all the unique characters you know. Take funny situations, mix in your one-of-a-kind family and friends, and add a dash of exaggeration. You may end up with more cartoon ideas than you could ever draw.

The cartoon above shows a common scene in most homes: a messy bedroom. Most of us think of our dirty laundry by category. I just took that idea and added a bit of exaggeration. I also think it's funny to see the kid trying to talk his way out of cleaning up. I do this all the time.

This is a classic example of Mom saying one thing and doing another. It happens all the time. Most people like to see the silly things they do reflected in cartoons. If a similar situation has happened to them, it's even funnier.

Making Jokes: A Step-By-Step Guide

1. Remember something funny that happened. Look for simple things that go wrong. Look for things that strike you as strange or funny. Perhaps start with a topic such as your pet, the school band, or gym class.

2. Take that idea and play with it. Exaggerate it, change it, and add things to it. Think of everything that relates to that subject. Make a long list and include some strange or surprising choices to spice things up.

3. Think of some silly, unexpected situations. Try taking a normal scene involving your subject and reversing something about it. Have fun and play with your ideas. There are no bad ideas here. Write down everything you think of. If you don't want to use your sketchpad to write down your jokes or ideas, carry an inexpensive notebook wherever you go.

4. Take your favorite ideas and write out your cartoons. Write down at least four or five ideas for each joke, and don't give up too easily.

5. Draw the best one. Begin the artistic process of planning, sketching, and inking your cartoon.

Humor Can Be Powerful

Cartoons should be used to make people laugh, tell good stories, or challenge people to think about something differently. You must remember, however, that cartoons should never be used to hurt someone's feelings. Drawing an ugly picture of someone and then calling that picture a cartoon is cowardly and unfair. Cartoonists, like superheroes, must use their powers for good. My own rule is that I don't make fun of anyone who is less powerful than I am. Give that some thought.

Joke Time

Here's an example of creating a joke from beginning to end. You lost the remote control to your television. Can we make that funny? Of course we can. Begin by writing down everything you can think of related to losing things. Then write down random ideas that exaggerate reality or mix in unrelated ideas about losing the TV remote. Choose a few of your favorite brainstormed ideas.

Now, start writing different versions of your brainstormed ideas. You may need to work through three or four versions of a joke before you get one that really makes you laugh. Don't give up too soon. Feel free to do rough sketches of your ideas as well.

We see a beach with several large, 30-foot-tall stone carvings of TV remotes facing the ocean. In the surf, we see a lone explorer pulling his boat onto the sand. The caption says, "Captain Fitzgerald fulfilled his lifelong ambition to locate the Island of Lost TV Remotes."

Kind of funny

A father is holding an armful of remote controls. He's explaining to the babysitter which one controls which entertainment device. He says, "This remote changes the volume. This remote changes the channel. This remote works the DVD player…and this remote finds the other remotes when they get lost."

Getting funnier

Draw a scene showing a living room, with mom talking to son. Mom is holding a TV remote. She says, "I finally found the TV remote…but now I've lost dad." We notice a man's leg and arm sticking out of the sofa cushions.

Once you have a cartoon you like, plan, sketch, and ink it. Decide what details make the cartoon strongest. If you can't decide which idea to run with, do more than one cartoon on your subject.

I've finally found the TV remote... but now I've lost dad.

Captions Needed!

Let's try something different. Below you'll find four different cartoons with no captions. Write as many funny lines as you can think of for each one. Write down ideas until you have four that you're really satisfied with. Make a copy of this page, and write the best caption under each cartoon. Now show them to your friends and family, and see whether you can make them laugh. It's not easy, but there's nothing better than getting that first laugh from something you wrote.

Comic Strips

Comic strips are a little different from single panel cartoons. More often than not, comic strips feature a continuing set of characters and story lines. You also have a little more space to set up your jokes. In a three- or four-panel comic strip, the first few panels set up the story, introduce a problem, or establish expectations. The last panel provides the surprise or joke. Generally, the punch line of a comic strip doesn't make much sense until you've read the panels that come before it. There's almost a rhythm to comic strip writing: setup, setup, joke.

Give your comic strip characters strong opinions and bold personalities! You'll find that the joke ideas will flow faster and more naturally.

Below are a few examples that illustrate how the initial panels can set up the joke. Notice how the writing flows, from setup to punch line.

Create Strong Comic Strip Characters

The most important thing to remember when writing a comic strip is to create good characters. It's a common mistake to say first, "I'd like to create a comic strip about superheroes." You may have a loose idea of a theme, but what you need are interesting characters. Because comic strips feature a recurring cast of characters, most of the jokes should flow from those characters' personalities.

Start with a basic personality type and keep getting more and more specific, until your character begins to take on his or her own unique personality. Here's an example:

Superhero. Pretty dull. It's been done a million times.

Really short superhero. Better, but still needs more.

Really grumpy, short superhero who hates cats. Now you're getting somewhere!

Invent the personalities first, and then figure out some theme or environment that they work well in. If your cartoon characters are truly unique, then they won't look or act like any other characters on the comics page. That's when you know you're on your way to creating a promising comic strip.

Chapter 8
Putting It All Together

WE'VE TALKED ABOUT ALL ASPECTS OF CARTOONING. We've covered tools, drawing basics, and even some tips on writing. Now we'll go step by step through the process of creating finished cartoons.

Let's assume your jokes have been written, and the punch lines are hilarious! Congratulations! It's time to put it all together.

Set Up Your Drawing Area

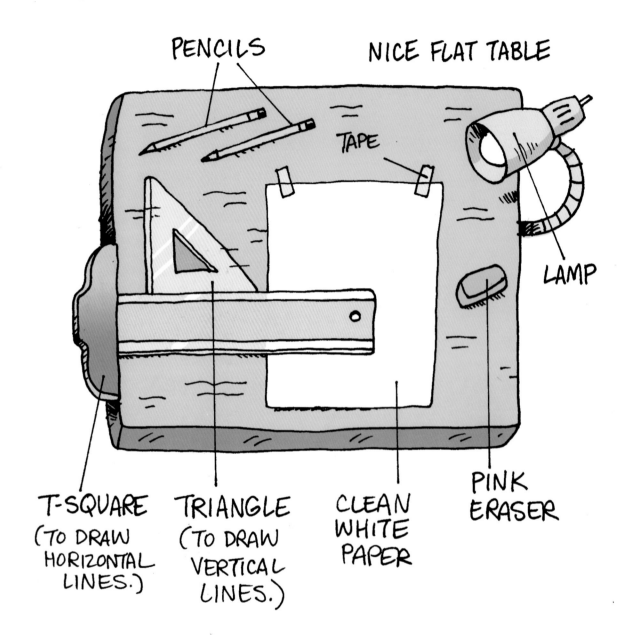

PENCILS

NICE FLAT TABLE

TAPE

LAMP

T-SQUARE
(TO DRAW
HORIZONTAL
LINES.)

TRIANGLE
(TO DRAW
VERTICAL
LINES.)

CLEAN
WHITE
PAPER

PINK
ERASER

Remember, you don't need to have an expensive drawing table to work on. Just find a smooth, flat surface with a straight edge along the left side. This is used to align the T-square, so you can make vertical and horizontal lines. You'll also need your paper, pencils, eraser, triangle, and some masking tape. It helps to have a lamp that gives off a bright, even light. Any small lamp will work fine.

Gag Cartoons

When creating finished, single-panel cartoons, you'll be using the three stages of cartooning discussed earlier: planning, sketching, and inking. Have your joke in your head or written down on paper. The planning stage is critical to figuring out what pieces are needed for the drawing and where you'll put them. Use the T-square and triangle to draw a square about 6 inches by 6 inches. Start planning and remember to draw very lightly, staying loose and messy.

You may do several planning layouts until you find the one that works best. Experiment until you find the one that's most effective. You'll know it when you see it.

Plan it!

Sketch it!

Ink it!

Placing Your Characters

In each of these cartoons the main character is placed on the right side, so the reader's focus will be on him. Your layout should guide the readers' eyes to the part of the drawing you want them to see.

Notice that the speaking character is standing, while the less important character is sitting. Again, this gives more importance to the speaker. The pink circles I've indicated on these cartoons let you know where I want the reader to look. When you plan your layout, think about where to place your invisible "bull's-eye."

Layout also determines the order in which things will be read. People in Western cultures read from left to right.

Notice how I've positioned the characters so that the reader first sees the scene, and then settles on my speaking character. This is where the layout becomes so important. And you thought cartooning was just doodling!

Cartoon Strips

In cartoon strips, the planning, sketching, and inking stages still apply, but you have to think about an effective layout for each frame in the cartoon. You also usually have more than one person talking, and the action takes place over time. With cartoon strips, it's helpful to think about your layout like the scene in a movie, with you as the director.

Above, you'll see two cartoon strip layouts. They both have the same exact action: two people talking. Notice how the one at the top is boring and repetitive. It's basically the same layout repeated three times. The second example is more interesting. It has a first frame that includes everything, a close-up of the speaking character in the second frame, and a silhouette in the last frame to add interest. Same joke, same action, but better layout.

Comic Books

Comic books present yet another set of challenges when it comes to layout and planning. The normal comic book page is read like sentences in a book. Starting from the upper left corner, the action flows across the page to the right, then moves down, then all the way back to the left side, then across to the right… over and over until you get to the bottom of the page. Each page needs to have a visual bull's-eye, but it shouldn't disrupt the flow of the action or dialogue.

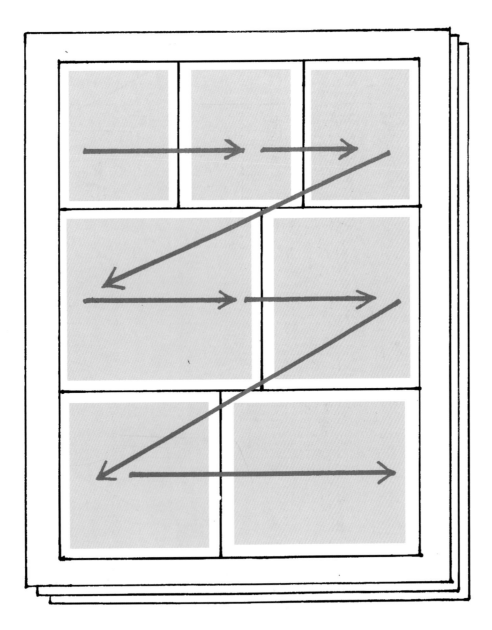

Remember to stay loose during the planning stage. Comic book pages can be a blast to design. Purchase a few comic books and study the way the artists change the layout to add drama and excitement.

As you can see in this example, a comic book page doesn't need to have the same size boxes lined up in a neat row. Try something different. Break out of boxes altogether. As long as you maintain a clear flow of action and story line, your comic book pages can look as wild as you want. Remember, you're writing a book with pictures.

Lettering

There's one thing we haven't touched on yet, and that's lettering. In most cartoons, the dialogue of the characters is displayed as text, in all capital letters, hand drawn by the cartoonist. It has been done this way since the beginning of cartooning itself. Some cartoonists today are using computers for their dialogue text, but I'll assume that you'll be using good old-fashioned pen and paper.

To add dialogue to your cartoons, start by measuring two horizontal lines, ¼ inch apart. Then move down ¹⁄₁₆ inch, and draw two more horizontal lines, ¼ inch apart. Keep doing this until you have enough lines to hold all the dialogue you've planned for that panel or page.

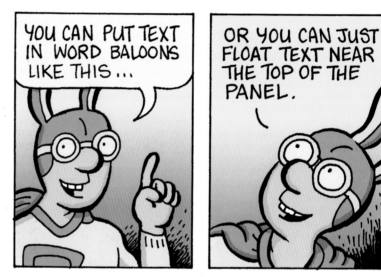

ABCDEFGHIJK
LMNOPQRSTU
VWXYZ
ABCDEFGHIJK
LMNOPQRSTU
VWXYZ.

This is an example my lettering style. I've written the entire alphabet so you can see how I draw each letter.

I've drawn some lettering guidelines here. Make a copy of these lines, and practice lettering the alphabet a few times. Before long, you'll have a lettering style to call your very own.

There are even different styles of word balloons, depending on what you're trying to accomplish.

Because cartooning tells a story using artwork, sometimes even your text can become part of the art. Here are some ways you can make sound effects stand out on the page. If you need to make an impact with sound, simply illustrate the sound in a big, loud cartoon-y way!

Coloring

Adding color to your cartoons is not difficult. Most of the illustrations in this book were colored right on my computer, using a program called Adobe Photoshop. On the next three pages you'll see three cartoon birds. I used a different method to color each one. The bird below was painted with watercolors. The bird on page 96 was done using colored pencils. I used the computer for the bird on page 97. Let's talk briefly about each of these methods.

Watercolor

Watercolors are paints that usually come in a tray filled with hardened blocks of pigment (or color). By dipping a small wet brush into each color, you can brush a small amount of watery paint onto your drawing. It's usually a good idea to paint on a copy rather than your original artwork in case you make a mistake.

It's also a good idea to pre-mix your colors on a small sheet of scrap paper before painting onto your drawing. Watercolor can be hard to master, but the materials are inexpensive, and it's a very fast way to add bright, smooth color.

Colored Pencils

Colored pencils offer more control than watercolors since they are dry and you can layer them one color on top of another. The drawback with pencils is that it's sometimes hard to get a really flat, bright color. Do some experiments and decide if you like the modeled texture you get with pencils. I really prefer it on some drawings. Always remember that when you're coloring your work, accidents can happen.

If you're only working on the photocopy, it's easy to start over with the color. If you mess up your original, you'll have to do the whole drawing over again!

The Computer

For the beginner, I would only recommend using the computer if you're already very comfortable using it for other tasks. The illustration on the right shows the type of computer set up I used in creating the color images for this book. If you want to add color to a drawing you did by hand, you'll need some way to get the drawing into the computer. A *scanner* is a device that takes a digital picture of your cartoon and puts it into the computer so you can open it up and add color. You'll need paint software (a computer program) to actually add the color. Most computers come with some sort of paint program pre-loaded, so see if your computer has something like this. The last item I used is optional, but it's called a *tablet*. This lets you use a pen to "paint" on the image instead of using the mouse. I prefer this method, but a mouse works just as well in most paint programs.

COMPUTER & PAINT SOFTWARE

PEN

TABLET

SCANNER

Just like when coloring by hand, it's a good idea to separate your color layer from your black lines layer in the paint program on the computer. That way, if you mess up the paint layer it doesn't harm the black lines layer.

Chapter 9
Publishing Your Cartoons

SO, YOU'VE CREATED A FINISHED CARTOON THAT MAKES YOU LAUGH. Maybe you have a lot of finished cartoons. Now what? It's time to get published. This is the last step in becoming a real cartoonist, and it can be the most exciting. There's a genuine feeling of satisfaction seeing your work in print, and it can be as easy as making some photocopies.

CHOONKA
CHOONKA
CHOONKA

Self-Publishing

Self-publishing is the fancy term for copying your cartoons on a photocopy machine. Using standard 8½ x 11-inch paper folded in half, you can manufacture little books of your cartoons to give to family and friends. You can even sell the books.

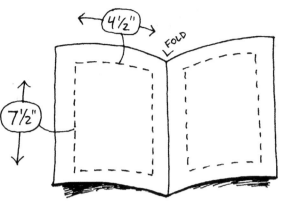

Lay out a standard sheet of paper horizontally. Determine the centerline by folding the paper in half so that the corners at the top and bottom meet. Unfold the paper and tape it to your table or drawing board. Now lightly sketch out an area, on each half of the paper, that's 4½ inches wide and 7½ inches tall. This will be the "live" area for your little book.

If you do single-panel cartoons, shrink your work to fit two cartoons per page, stacked one on top of the other. You can handwrite the captions or type them out on a computer and paste them below each cartoon. Play with the reduction settings on the copier until you have a size that works.

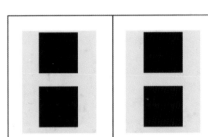

If you do cartoon strips, simply shrink your cartoons on a copier until they are 4½ inches wide, and then cut and paste them onto your pages. You may be able to fit three strips into each 4½ x 7½-inch area. Another option with comic strips is to turn the cartoons sideways and use only one per page.

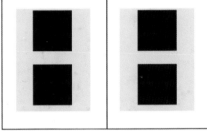

If you do comic-book-style cartoons, your job is easy. Reduce each full page until it fits within your 4½ x 7½-inch area. If you plan ahead, you can design the size of your pages to reduce perfectly into this space.

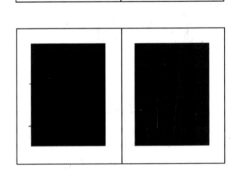

After you've pasted down all your cartoons, stack the pages together. Fold them in half, and you have an instant 5½ x 8½-inch book. After stacking them together, you may notice that every other page in your book is empty. This is because you pasted cartoons onto only one side of each layout sheet. If you'd like a book with cartoons on every page, just use the front and back of each layout sheet before stacking the pages together. You'll have fewer pages but no blank spaces!

Cover Up

Every book needs a cover. Add one more page to your stack, and design a cover for your book on the right half of the layout sheet. If you want, you can create your cover illustration in full color, then have this page color copied separately from the rest of your book.

Add all the copied pages together, fold them neatly, and add two staples to the binding to hold the book together. Do this for each of your copies. Some copy shops will do this production work for you. Just bring in the color cover design and all the cartoons pasted down onto layout pages. They'll do the copying, folding, and stapling for you. However, they do charge for this service.

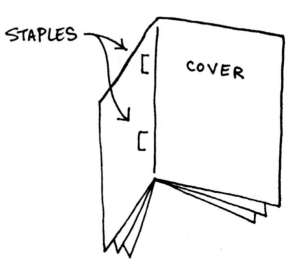

Local Publications

You'd be surprised by how many opportunities there are to get your cartoons published right in your own town. The secret is to create cartoons with subject matter that's specially geared to each publication you approach. For a school newspaper, do cartoons about your school—the football team, the school lunch, etc. Keep your eyes open for opportunities to be published. There are free weekly papers and small flyers and newsletters everywhere. Here are a few ideas for local publications:

- School newspapers
- School newsletters
- Church newsletters
- School yearbooks

- Free weekly newspapers
- Advertising newspapers
- Corporate newsletters
- Local businesses/restaurants

Don't expect to be paid for your work. The small publications you'll be calling on might not have the money to pay cartoonists. What you're looking for is experience.

Sell Yourself

Here are some tips on letting local publications know you have cartoons you'd like them to publish:

1. Get out there and visit them.

2. Do your research. Find out the name of the editor for each publication you want to approach. Call and make an appointment to show your work.

3. When you visit, don't bring in original artwork. Instead, show clean, neat copies, and have enough so you can leave a few behind.

3. Create a folder of the cartoons you want to show. An organized presentation will help show that you are a professional, and that will go a long way toward getting people to take you seriously.

4. Put your name and contact information on each cartoon.

JOE SMITH 555-4279

5. Stress the fact that you're not expecting payment. For the beginning cartoonist, getting published is your primary goal.

6. Show cartoons that cover subject matters specific to each publication. For church bulletins, offer cartoons about the choir or church parking problems. For local free papers, show cartoons about local politics or local environmental issues.

7. After your cartoons appear in print, remember to collect several samples of the publication for your files. As you gain experience, it's important to have examples of published work to show to other potential clients.

National Publications

There are many opportunities for publishing in national magazines. Again, getting paid may be optional here. For the beginner, target magazines and publications that cater to kids. Go to the library or newsstand and look through these kid magazines very carefully. Look for sections devoted to reader-based cartoon submissions and for magazines with comic sections.

Don't hesitate to send your work off to comic book companies such as DC and Marvel Comics. The odds are stacked against you because you'll be competing against seasoned professionals, but there is valuable experience to be gained by submitting your cartoons for review, particularly if the submission results in some feedback about your work. Any advice you can get about your cartoons will make you a better cartoonist. This is all part of your education as a cartoonist.

Comic Strips

Companies called *newspaper syndicates* distribute the comic strips that you see in newspapers. There are a few large syndicates, including King Features, Universal Press, and United Media. Research these syndicates at the library or on the Internet. Look at a magazine called *Editor & Publisher* to find out more about the syndication business. Here, too, the odds are stacked against you, because these syndicates get thousands of comic strip ideas sent to them each year. If comic strips are what you want to do, then just keep trying.

What You Do

Create a sample pack of your cartoons to send off in the mail. Include 24 cartoons, neatly copied onto 8½ x 11-inch white paper. Remember to include your name and contact information on each page. You'll also want to include a short two-paragraph introductory letter that explains who you are and what type of cartoons you do.

Sending off cartoons to national publications is kind of like putting a message in a bottle and throwing it into the ocean. You never know when you're going to get a response. Generally, though, if you haven't received a phone call or a letter after six weeks, you can call and ask about your submission. Remind them who you are and what you sent.

If you do get a letter back, and your cartoons have been turned down for publication, don't worry. Even professional cartoonists get these notices all the time. They're called rejection letters. After you get one of these, you KNOW you're a real cartoonist! Keep working to make your cartoons better, and don't stop sending cartoons to publications. Be persistent. Eventually you will be published, and it will feel fantastic.

Chapter 10
Draw, Draw, Draw!

I HOPE THAT AFTER READING THIS BOOK YOU'VE DISCOVERED THE CARTOONIST we both know is inside you. But remember that even the most famous cartoonists were not born that way. They had to work pretty hard to get better. They continue to read and learn about other cartoonists, and they are always up for trying new things. Most of all, the great cartoonists draw all the time. They do this because they love it, and because they know that this is the one and only way to improve their skills.

Draw on the school bus. Draw in front of the TV. Draw INSTEAD of watching TV! Draw silly cartoons and leave them around the house for your family. Create one character and draw him doing everything you can think of.

You probably already like to draw, or you wouldn't be reading this book. Save some special time each day just for cartooning. When you can't think of a cartoon idea, just draw your favorite original character. If you don't have an original character, spend some time trying to create one. If you don't feel like doing that, just draw whatever's in front of you!

Sometimes you need to draw three or four cartoons to get warmed up, so don't make the mistake of quitting early. Stick with it and draw for at least a half hour every day.

The important thing to remember is...not every cartoon has to be a masterpiece. For a beginner, it's better to create 20 so-so drawings than three great ones.

On the next page you'll find a fun grid that you can use for drawing challenges. If you get stuck for an idea, use the grid to create a different cartoon drawing assignment every day for 30 days.

Cartoonumator Grid Challenge

Create your own cartoon practice assignment by choosing one piece of the description out of each column. Try to pick off-the-wall combinations that will offer a unique, fun challenge.

Example: 1C - 2J - 3L - 4A = Four fluffy sheep holding a hammer, running at full speed while juggling three table lamps.

	①	②	③	④
A	A spotted cow...	wearing a large cowboy hat...	and riding a bicycle...	while juggling three table lamps.
B	A giant, angry bee...	waving a flag...	and driving a speed boat...	and eating a sandwich.
C	Four fluffy sheep...	holding bottles of soda...	made of glass...	while a plane flies overhead.
D	A well-dressed man...	holding a sword...	riding in a convertible...	and blowing a bubble gum bubble.
E	A slimy frog...	yelling at a bird...	and riding a pony...	sitting on a tree stump.
F	Two barefoot cowboys...	in a football helmet..	out in a swamp...	flying a kite.
G	A knight in armor...	talking on the phone...	stuck in quicksand...	and playing a bongo drum.
H	A beautiful mermaid...	selling lemonade...	smiling with a missing tooth...	screaming, "I need a hug!"
I	A skinny dog...	eating popcorn...	soaking wet...	jumps into a small pond.
J	An ugly, three headed alien...	holding a hammer...	and waving to the crowd...	eating ice cream.
K	A crying elephant...	singing a song...	and dancing on a table...	says, "Howdy pardner!"
L	A goldfish...	reading a book...	running full speed...	and falling fast asleep.
M	A one-eyed pirate...	on roller skates...	flying through the air...	and singing opera.

Final Thoughts from Bunny Guy

There are other simple drawing games that you can play with a friend. Start with a blank piece of paper and ask your friend to draw the shape of a head. Then you try to complete the face. Keep going back and forth, taking turns, until you've completed an entire character.

Or ask a friend to guess who you're drawing. Start drawing a cartoon of someone you both know, and see how many guesses it takes for your friend to get it right. The point is that drawing can be fun alone or with friends.

Whatever you do, keep drawing. I sometimes go through my old sketchbooks and get great ideas for cartoons just by looking at doodles and silly drawings. Keep a sketchbook the way other people might keep a diary. Carry it with you. Open it and use it whenever you can. Soon you'll completely fill up every page, and then you can start on your second sketchbook, and then your third and your fourth. Your sketchbooks are the visual history of your growth as a cartoonist.

Good luck in your new life as a cartoonist. Now put down this book and keep drawing!

Acknowledgments

I'd like to acknowledge the hard work of Joe Rhatigan and Celia Naranjo at Lark Books. A big thanks to Joanne O'Sullivan for thinking of me for this project. Thanks also to my wife Elizabeth for her never-ending patience and encouragement.

I dedicate this book to the memory of my mother, Ellen O'Flaherty Roche. She saw an early spark, and took me to art lessons even when I didn't want to go.

www.artroche.com
Check it out!

Index